Dear Parents and Educators,

Welcome to Penguin Young Readers! As parents
know that each child develops at his or her own
speech, critical thinking, and, of course, reading. Penguin Young
Readers recognizes this fact. As a result, each Penguin Young Readers
book is assigned a traditional easy-to-read level (1–4) as well as a
Guided Reading Level (A–P). Both of these systems will help you choose
the right book for your child. Please refer to the back of each book
for specific leveling information. Penguin Young Readers features
esteemed authors and illustrators, stories about favorite characters,
fascinating nonfiction, and more!

Spacesuits

LEVEL **3**

GUIDED
READING
LEVEL **M**

This book is perfect for a **Transitional Reader** who:
- can read multisyllable and compound words;
- can read words with prefixes and suffixes;
- is able to identify story elements (beginning, middle, end, plot, setting, characters, problem, solution); and
- can understand different points of view.

Here are some **activities** you can do during and after reading this book:
- Nonfiction: Nonfiction books deal with facts and events that are real. Talk about the elements of nonfiction. Then, on a separate sheet of paper, write down some of the facts you learned about spacesuits.
- Creative Writing: Imagine you are an astronaut getting ready to go to space. How would you prepare? What would you bring with you? Write a paragraph about all the things you would see and do.

Remember, sharing the love of reading with a child is the best gift
you can give!

—Sarah Fabiny, Editorial Director
  Penguin Young Readers program

*Penguin Young Readers are leveled by independent reviewers applying the standards developed by Irene Fountas
and Gay Su Pinnell in *Matching Books to Readers: Using Leveled Books in Guided Reading*, Heinemann, 1999.

PENGUIN YOUNG READERS
An Imprint of Penguin Random House LLC

● Smithsonian
This trademark is owned by the Smithsonian Institution and is registered
in the U.S. Patent and Trademark Office.

Smithsonian Enterprises:
Christopher Liedel, President
Carol LeBlanc, Senior Vice President, Education and Consumer Products
Brigid Ferraro, Vice President, Education and Consumer Products
Ellen Nanney, Licensing Manager
Kealy Gordon, Product Development Manager

National Air and Space Museum, Smithsonian:
Cathleen S. Lewis, Curator, International Space Programs and Spacesuits, Department of Space History

Photo credits: NASA: pages 6, 7, 9, 10, 11, 13, 15, 18 (bottom), 19, 22, 23, 24, 25, 26, 27, 28, 29, 30, 31, 32.
Smithsonian National Air and Space Museum: pages 3, 4, 8, 14, 16, 17, 18 (top), 20.
Text copyright © 2017 by Penguin Random House LLC and Smithsonian Institution. All rights reserved.
Published by Penguin Young Readers, an imprint of Penguin Random House LLC, 345 Hudson Street,
New York, New York 10014. Manufactured in China.

Library of Congress Cataloging-in-Publication Data is available.

ISBN 9780515157758 (pbk)
ISBN 9780515157765 (hc)

10 9 8 7 6 5 4 3 2 1
10 9 8 7 6 5 4 3 2 1

☀ Smithsonian
SPACESUITS

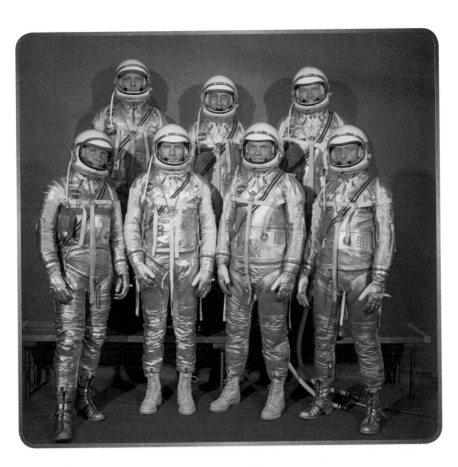

by James Buckley Jr.

Penguin Young Readers
An Imprint of Penguin Random House

Gemini 3 suit, March 1965

Contents

Spacecraft for One

What do you wear to work when it's colder than a freezer, or hotter than boiling water, and there's no air?

A spacesuit!

Spacesuits make travel beyond
Earth possible. They're a one-person
spacecraft!

John Glenn wore this suit on February 20, 1962,
when he became the first American to orbit Earth.

People first went into space in the
1960s. They wore spacesuits on these
rocket rides.

8

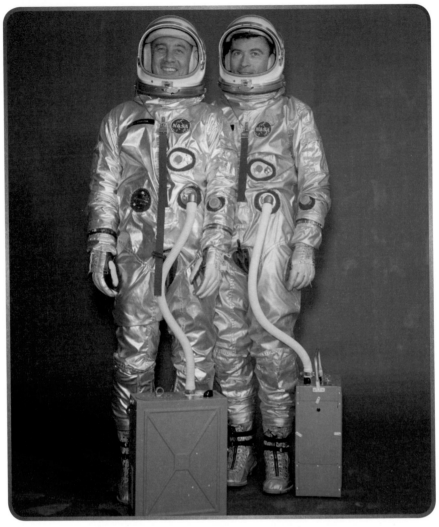

Gemini 3 crew and their air supply, 1964

The suits plugged into an air supply in the spacecraft. Spacesuits are sealed so the air cannot escape.

On June 3, 1965, Ed White became the first American to walk in space. Spacewalking astronauts needed thicker suits to protect them.

Today, astronauts on the **International Space Station**, or ISS, wear similar spacesuits to work outside. ISS spacesuits are much heavier. The legs are also stiffer because ISS astronauts do not have to walk.

Ed White walking in space

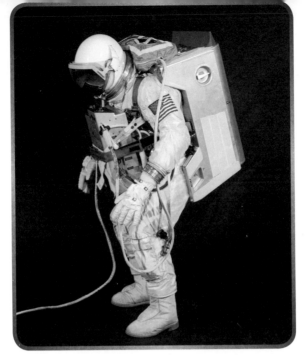

Spacewalking suit, 1966

ISS astronaut Karen Nyberg, 2013

Layers for Living

Spacesuits today are made of up to 14 layers of material. Some layers keep in heat so the astronaut stays warm. Others keep out the sun's strong energy. The astronaut does not want to get too warm!

All the layers help protect the astronaut outside the spacecraft. They could get hit by tiny, tiny flying bits of asteroids or comets!

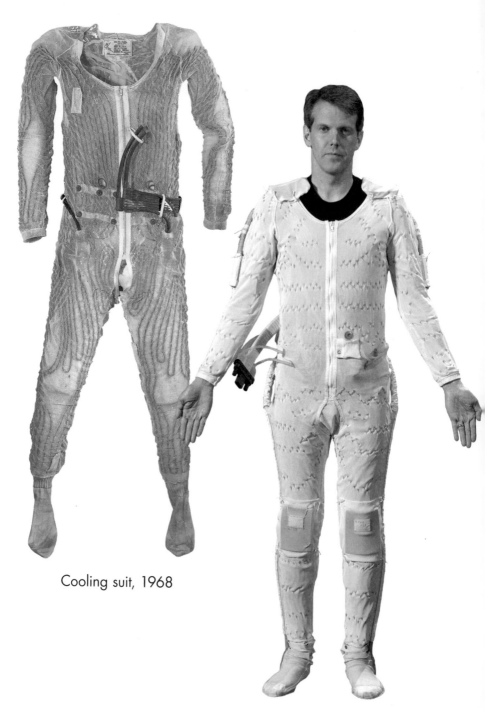

Cooling suit, 1968

Cooling suit, 2006

Keeping Cool

Working in a heavy, bulky spacesuit is hot! The sun's rays add even more heat.

To stay cool, astronauts wear a special suit under their spacesuit. It is made of thin, stretchy material covered with tubes. Cool water flows through these tubes. This keeps the astronaut comfortable.

Astronauts wear special underwear, too!

Give Them a Hand

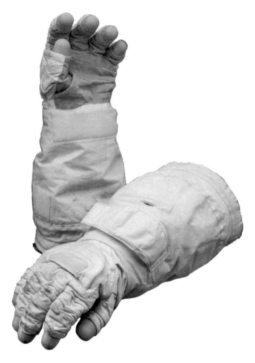

Astronaut Kathryn D. Sullivan, first American woman
to walk in space, wore these gloves in 1984.

Gloves protect an astronaut's
hands. The fingertips have special
caps. This makes grabbing small
things easier.

Gloves worn by **cosmonauts** on the ISS, 2016

The gloves also have heaters in the fingertips.
Metal rings seal the gloves to the spacesuit.

Helmet Head

Spacesuit helmets include a lot of key gear. The helmet has a clear **visor** to see through. Astronauts can pull

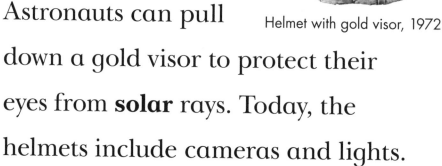

Helmet with gold visor, 1972

down a gold visor to protect their eyes from **solar** rays. Today, the helmets include cameras and lights.

Helmet with lights and visor, 2013

Astronaut Mae Jemison in a "Snoopy Cap" and helmet, 1992

Under the helmet, astronauts wear a "Snoopy Cap." It is named after the famous cartoon dog.

This cap has earphones and a microphone. It connects to the radio in the spacesuit.

ISS astronaut Mike Hopkins in a "Snoopy Cap," 2013

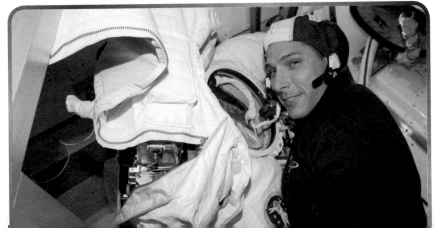

Backpack for Breathing

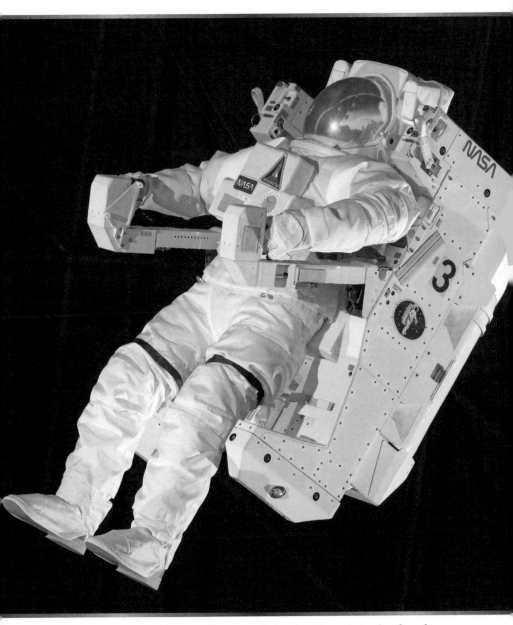

Astronaut Bruce McCandless used this backpack in the first free "flying" spacewalk, 1984

Astronauts outside a spacecraft wear backpacks with something very special inside: air!

Inhale!

The equipment inside the backpack provides **oxygen**.

Exhale!

It removes bad gases from the air when the astronauts breathe out.

The backpack runs the spacesuit's radio, lights, cameras, and fans that move air around inside the suit. Some backpacks include mini-jets. Then the astronaut can "fly" instead of just float.

Getting Dressed

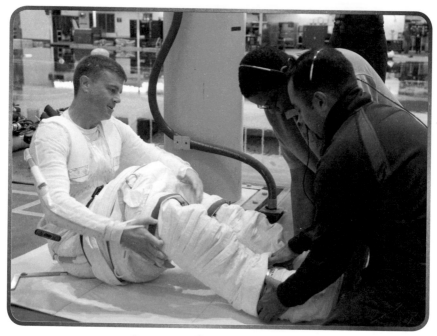

Suiting up for training, 2012

Getting dressed for space takes teamwork! During training, helpers put each part of the suit on an astronaut.

In space, astronauts help one another. The different parts of the suit click together.

Suiting up to walk in space, 2007.

The spacesuit's **torso** is **rigid** so it can hold important controls. The astronaut can push buttons on the front. The arms are attached to this section. Then the helmet goes on.

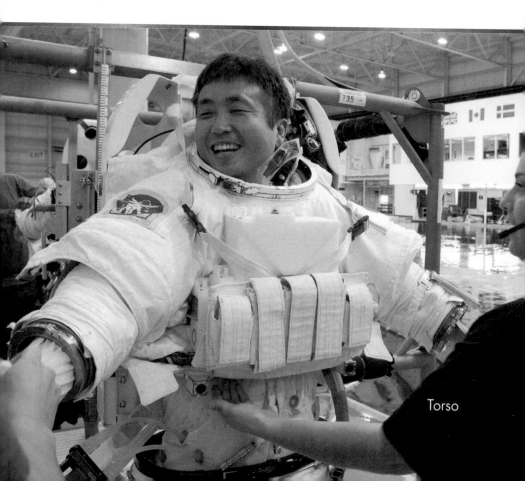

Torso

Arms, gloves, and helmet

Thumbs up . . . ready to go!

Take a Walk

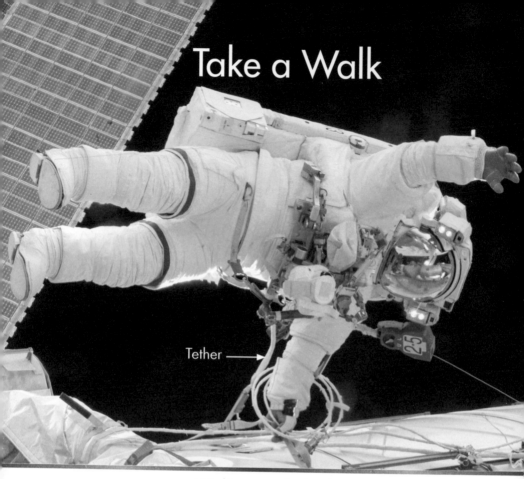

Tether ⟶

Working outside the ISS

When astronauts work outside, they put on their complete spacesuits. This includes backpacks and tools.

Tethers connect the suit to the station, and the tools to the astronauts. That way, nothing—and nobody—will float away!

Tether

Tether

Another Way to Fly

Astronauts wear spacesuits during launches, flights, or spacewalks. They have to in order to breathe and stay safe.

But inside the space station, they can relax. It's warm inside. There's air. Comfy clothes rule! But slippers, socks, or sneakers only. Hard shoes might damage station gear.

Packing for Space

Astronauts sometimes bring famous objects with them into space. Or they bring things to give to friends and family when they return.

The Olympic torch on the ISS, 2013

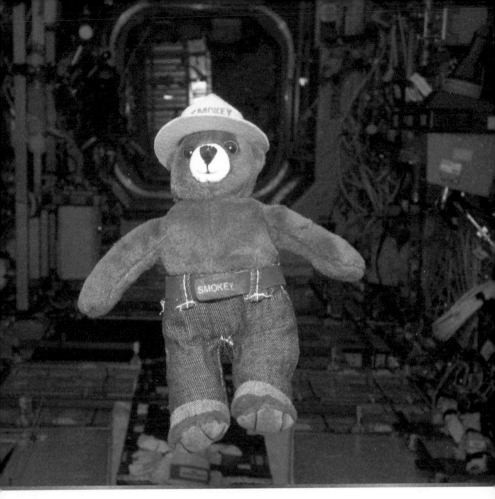

Smokey Bear doll on the ISS, 2012

Some space **souvenirs** are
on display at the Smithsonian
National Air and Space Museum in
Washington, DC. They're truly out of
this world!

cosmonauts: name for space travelers from Russia

International Space Station (ISS): a spacecraft built by 11 nations that orbits Earth

oxygen: a gas we breathe that has no smell or color

rigid: stiff, unbending

souvenirs: objects that remind you of someone, something, or someplace

solar: having to do with the sun

tethers: lines or wires that connect objects

torso: the upper body of a person, between the waist and neck, but not including the arms or head

visor: a covering that shades or protects the face